51

SCOUTS
OF THE WILD WEST

Jeff Savage

ENSLOW PUBLISHERS, INC.
44 Fadem Road   P.O. Box 38
Box 699   Aldershot
Springfield, N.J. 07081   Hants GU12 6BP
U.S.A.   U.K.

Library of Congress Cataloging-in-Publication Data

Savage, Jeff, 1961–
     Scouts of the Wild West / Jeff Savage.
          p. cm. — (Trailblazers of the Wild West)
     Includes bibliographical references and index.
     ISBN 0-89490-605-4
          1. Scouts and scouting—West (U.S.)—History—19th century—Juvenile
literature. 2. West (U.S.)—Social life and customs—Juvenile literature. [1. Scouts
and scouting—West (U.S.) 2. Frontier and pioneer life—West (U.S.)] I. Title. II. Series.
F596.S2357 1995
978'.02'0922—dc20   94-33361
                                                                        CIP
                                                                        AC
Printed in the United States of America

10 9 8 7 6 5 4 3 2 1

Illustration Credits: Arizona Historical Society Library, p. 29; Denver
Public Library, Western History Department, pp. 9, 10, 11, 12, 27, 28, 34, 39,
43; Engraving by John C. Buttre, *Dictionary of American Portraits* (Dover
Publications, Inc., 1967), p. 35; Kansas State Historical Society, p. 41; Library
of Congress, pp. 6, 32, 36; Courtesy Library of Congress Brady-Handy
Collection, p. 18; Kristin McCarthy, p. 13; Nebraska State Historical Society,
p. 24; Nevada Historical Society, p. 20.

Cover Illustration: Paul Daly

CONTENTS

1 Kit and the Bear   5

2 The First Scouts   8

3 Pioneer Scouts 17

4 Scouting for the Army Corps 22

5 Jim Bridger and Kit Carson 30

6 The End of the Scout 38

Notes by Chapter 44

Glossary 45

Further Reading 46

Index 47

❖❖ 1 ❖❖

KIT AND THE BEAR

———◆•◈•◆———

Kit Carson raised his rifle, took careful aim, and—*bang!*—blasted a bullet right into the elk. The animal collapsed to the ground, dead on the spot. Kit was pleased to have bagged some food at last. It had been several days since he and his trapper friends had eaten meat.

Kit was a twenty-six-year-old explorer working as a scout in the Black Hills of what is now South Dakota. The year was 1835, and the land in which Kit found himself was part of the howling wilderness of the West. Only a handful of white people knew much about the land west of the Mississippi River, or about how to survive in such terrain. Kit Carson was one of them.

The trappers for whom Kit worked had been hunting for soft beaver pelts. It was Kit's responsibility as scout to be the eyes and ears of his group. He had to guide the trappers through rugged country, fetch food for them, and keep them from harm. What's more, there were plenty of ferocious animals prowling about, as Kit was about to discover.

Kit leaned over to inspect the dead elk. All at once, he heard a terrific roar from behind. He snapped his head around, and there they were—two big grizzly bears, charging right at him! Kit had already fired his gun, and he had no time to reload it. He spotted a nearby pine tree and made a run for it. The grizzlies—in hot pursuit—were at his feet when he reached the tree. Kit dropped his gun and leaped to the safety of a tree limb

Kit Carson and the trappers in camp.

just in time. "I had to drop my gun—the bears rushing for me, I had to make all haste to ascend the tree," Kit later explained.[1]

With his gun lying on the ground at the grizzlies' feet, Kit had no choice but to sit in the tree and hope that the bears would leave. One grizzly lost interest quickly, but the other stayed. It pawed at Kit, who couldn't climb any higher. To protect himself, Kit broke off a tree branch, and used it to hit the bear on the snout each time it got too close. The bear snarled and growled. The sky grew dark as night arrived. It wasn't until midnight that the grizzly got bored and wandered away. Kit dropped down from the tree, picked up his gun, and dashed the mile back to camp.

The trappers were thrilled to see Kit. They had feared that he was lost, or worse, dead. Kit told them about the grizzly bears, and said that he had never been "so scared in all my life."[2] With the bears still lurking in the darkness, Kit didn't dare to go back for the elk. The trappers wouldn't have meat for supper again that night, but they didn't mind. Their scout was safe.

Kit had always wanted to be a scout. He grew up listening to stories about Daniel Boone, a scout from Kentucky. Even before the Declaration of Independence was written in 1776, Boone was making history in America as a great explorer. He blazed a trail known as the Wilderness Road. Young Kit wanted to be a frontiersman like Daniel Boone.

❧ 2 ❧

THE FIRST SCOUTS

When the first white settlers arrived in America they met both friendly and unfriendly Native Americans. Many settlers, such as the Pilgrims of Massachusetts, might not have survived without the help of Native Americans. Later, in the French and Indian War, eastern Native Americans took sides and served as guides for both the French and the British. The British and American troops in the Revolutionary War were led once again by Native American scouts.

When the United States purchased Louisiana from France in 1803, the new nation nearly tripled in size. To back up its claim, the United States needed to settle the land quickly. The government encouraged people to establish homes in the frontier. At that time, however, western North America was still mostly unexplored by white settlers.

A lithograph from the 1800s shows the many facets of scout life. Featured at top is Yellowstone Kelly.

Meanwhile, the Native Americans had been living on this land for thousands of years, and many of them did not welcome the westward expansion of white settlers. The Native Americans wanted to keep their land, eventually fighting settlers and soldiers in hundreds of bloody skirmishes. Yet the first scouts to lead the expansion were Native Americans.

Sacajawea

One of the first American expeditions through the West was led by a Native American—Sacajawea. Explorers Meriwether Lewis and William Clark are famous for their travels through the Pacific Northwest in 1804–1805.

Sacajawea has been honored all over the West with statues such as this one in Portland, Oregon.

President Thomas Jefferson commissioned Meriwether Lewis and William Clark to explore the newly purchased Louisiana Territory in 1804.

Their names might not be known today if not for the help of Sacajawea.

Sacajawea was a Shoshoni woman who had been purchased and married by a French-Canadian frontiersman named Toussaint Charbonneau. With Pomp, their newborn son, Sacajawea and Charbonneau joined the Lewis and Clark expedition. Charbonneau was hired as an interpreter, and Sacajawea was hired as a guide.

The mere presence of Sacajawea and her baby saved the Lewis and Clark expedition from attack countless times. Native Americans knew upon seeing a woman and a baby, that the group was not a war party. Eventually, the expedition reached its goal—the Pacific Ocean.

A year later, explorers Zebulon Pike and Stephen H. Long began leading U.S. army expeditions through the same wilderness the Lewis and Clark expedition had traveled.

Early Scouting

The tales of early scouts spread through the towns of the eastern United States. People soon realized the significance of the land west of the Mississippi River and began to head west. They knew about the dangers that lurked in the vastness of the West, but they knew little about the land itself. For instance, the pioneers in the first wagon train to the West Coast in 1841 knew only that Oregon lay somewhere to the west. They did not

Zebulon Pike (1779–1813) was an early explorer of the West. Pike's Peak in Colorado was named in his honor.

know how long the trip would take, nor did they know whether they would survive the rugged mountains or scorching deserts along the way. Scouts were needed more than ever.

Trappers joined Native Americans in providing their services to whoever hired them. Many of them lived among the Native Americans and had adapted to their ways of life. The Native Americans taught the trappers

Scouts first blazed the paths that would become the California and Oregon Trails in the 1830s. California was still part of Mexico, and the Oregon Country was up for grabs between the United States and Great Britain.

how to survive on their own. These skills were invaluable to the pioneers.

Though white settlers poured into the west by the thousands, many Native Americans were not hostile to them. White scouts traded, worked with, and even lived in the villages of Native Americans. They became blood brothers, married Native American women, and sometimes were declared chiefs.

To do all this, scouts had to communicate with the Native Americans. There were dozens of Native American nations, and each had a different spoken language. It was impossible to learn so many languages, so scouts and Native Americans used sign language, making signals with fingers and hands.

Duties of the Scouts

Scouts were responsible for the safety of the people they were leading westward. They served as a vital resource for the survival of both explorers and pioneers. They were the eyes and ears of these groups.

Some of the things they would be called upon to do included:

❖ Keeping a sharp eye open for signs of danger.
❖ Finding the safest route and sticking to it.
❖ Finding ways to cover their tracks.
❖ Persuading expedition leaders to follow their advice.
❖ Locating food and clean water for settlers and horses.

❖ Hunting and fighting off dangerous animals.

❖ Carrying urgent messages.

❖ Translating for Native Americans.

Scouts examined the ground and found clues that saved the people they were guiding from attack. They marked their way through barren plains. They made clever decisions about when to travel and when to hide.

Food

Food was sometimes difficult to come by. Bread, for instance, was nonexistent. Kit Carson ate bread about once a year. A scout named Jim Bridger went seven years without bread. Another scout survived for seventeen years without a single piece of bread. Fruits and vegetables were also scarce in such places as the Mojave Desert and the Rocky Mountains. The only food that almost always was available was meat, so scouts ate plenty of it, often consuming ten pounds a day.

What if there were no animals to hunt? Scouts survived as best they could. A desparate scout would cut his horse to draw blood, add water to the blood, and drink it as soup. If things got worse, he would kill the horse and eat it. When that option wasn't available, scouts would eat anything that crawled. They munched on spiders, grasshoppers, and worms. Scouts who crossed barren stretches of sand often had to devour a stew of black desert crickets. One scout even recalled plunging his arm into swarming anthills and then licking off the insects.

Major General Grenville Dodge, a chief engineer for the Union Pacific Railroad, worked with many scouts. Dodge wrote:

> *Nothing escaped their vision. The dropping of a stick or breaking of a twig, the turning of the growing grass all brought knowledge to them, and they could tell who or what had done it. Their methods of hunting game were perfect and we were never out of meat. Herbs, roots, berries, bark of trees and everything that was edible they knew. They could minister to the sick, dress wounds—in fact in all my experience I never saw [them] meet any obstacle they could not overcome.*[1]

❈ 3 ❈

PIONEER SCOUTS

Scouts often rode several miles ahead of their party to ensure the safety of the route. A scout named Thomas "Broken Hand" Fitzpatrick once had a terrifying experience while he was riding alone in the Rocky Mountains. (He became known as Broken Hand after a rifle accidentally discharged and shattered his wrist.)

Broken Hand was guiding a group of men through a rugged area known as South Pass. Broken Hand was a few miles ahead of the group when he came across a Gros Ventre war party. The Gros Ventre lived in what is now eastern Idaho. The warriors spotted Broken Hand on his horse, and the chase was on. Broken Hand's horse galloped over boulders and through ravines until it could go no farther. The Gros Ventre were still right behind. Broken Hand jumped off his horse and ran, clutching his rifle up a mountain of solid rock. He found a crack in the rock and squirmed in, then quickly covered the opening with leaves. The Gros Ventre searched along the mountainside for Broken Hand, coming within inches of him, but they could not find him. They knew that he could not go far without his horse, and that eventually he would have to come out of hiding. So the Gros Ventre built a campsite at the base of the rock mountain, and they waited. Broken Hand lay still for three days and nights. He was trapped.

Broken Hand had no food or water; he knew he had to escape. On the fourth night, he decided to make a run for it. He crawled out from the crevice and crept down the mountain. Miraculously, the Gros Ventre did not

Father Pierre Jean De Smet (1801-1873) was a Belgian missionary. Broken Hand Fitzpatrick led De Smet and his fellow missionaries to the Oregon Country.

hear him. He could not see in the dark, but because he was such a good scout, he still figured out where he was. He began a long journey to Pierre's Hole, which was the original destination of his group. The next day, he arrived at the swift-flowing Snake River. To cross it, Broken Hand used a small boat that he built from tree branches. Halfway across, the boat smashed into a rock. Broken Hand managed to swim safely to the other side, but he lost his lone remaining possession—his rifle—in the river.

For the next five days, Broken Hand staggered along toward Pierre's Hole. He stopped occasionally to rest and to dig up roots for food. His moccasins had worn off, and his feet were bloody and sore. He tore his leather hat into strips and wrapped them around his feet. At one point, he found himself cornered by a pack of hungry wolves. They charged him, and he escaped by climbing a tree. As he sat in the tree, a buffalo happened by. The buffalo was attacked by the wolves and was killed. When the wolves finally wandered away, Broken Hand dropped from the tree. He ate some raw buffalo meat, then trudged on. He went as far as he could until he collapsed from exhaustion.

When Broken Hand was found the next day by a pair of men who had been sent to look for him, he was near death. Pierre's Hole was just a few miles away. The men carried him back to camp, where he was nursed back to health. It was quite an ordeal, and Broken Hand's

Scout James Beckwourth was born a slave in Virginia in 1798. In 1848, he established a route through the Sierra Nevadas.

appearance proved it. When he first encountered the Gros Ventre two weeks earlier, his hair was brown. The incredible journey had turned his hair white. Broken Hand was given a new nickname—"White Hair."

No scout found any satisfaction in a wild pursuit such as this. There always was a bright side for scouts—during their wild journeys, they sometimes discovered a new trail. Getting credit for such a discovery, however, was another matter.

Elisha Stevens, Isaac Hitchcock, and Caleb Greenwood

Elisha Stevens, Isaac Hitchcock, and Caleb Greenwood were three scouts who discovered the California Trail in

1844. This trail was an old Native American path that split off from the Oregon Trail and went southwest through the Sierra Nevadas to the gold country of northern California. Stevens, Hitchcock, and Greenwood spread the word about this trail. Thousands of emigrants soon began using the route to reach the gold fields, yet these three men were barely recognized for their achievement.

Jesse Applegate and Moses Harris

Jesse Applegate and Moses Harris led a scouting party that forged a new route from the California Trail to southern Oregon. The route broke from the trail at the Humboldt River in Utah, and wound northwest through the Cascade Mountains. For some reason, Harris gained no fame for his part in creating the new route. It became known only as Applegate's Cutoff.

4

SCOUTING FOR THE ARMY CORPS

In 1836, the government created a small but resourceful army unit known as the Corps of Topographical Engineers. These men were responsible for mapping the vast western territory. Eventually every mountain and river was accounted for.

The corps inspected mountain passes to find routes that wagon trains could use to travel and where railroad tracks could be laid. The corps searched for areas containing supplies of water, food, and grasses in which to build forts. For a quarter of a century these army engineers studied millions of square miles of land. They couldn't have done it without the help of the scouts who led them.

Antoine Leroux

Among the most famous scouts for the corps was

Antoine Leroux. He helped guide teams of engineers along the cliffs of the southern Rockies and through the deserts of the Southwest. Antoine's first assignment in 1846 was to lead a corps group commanded by Captain Philip Cooke. The corps was looking for a wagon route from Santa Fe, New Mexico, to San Diego, near the Pacific Ocean. The problem was that the Rocky Mountains were in the way. Antoine said he could find another way to get to San Diego, and so they set off.

Antoine wanted the corps to go south along the Rio Grande for 230 miles, then southwest into Mexico for another 160 miles to get through the mountains at Guadalupe Pass. Captain Cooke agreed to this plan at first. Antoine traveled more than fifty miles ahead of the corps as he searched for water and for ground smooth enough for wagons to roll across. He would communicate with the corps by using smoke signals or by leaving notes attached to trees.

The corps traveled for more than a month, and Captain Cooke was getting more frustrated each day. He was in too much of a hurry. He didn't like the idea of going around the mountains. Why not just cut through them?

Antoine waited for the corps on the trail one day. He had good news: Guadalupe Pass was just one more day away. Captain Cooke didn't care. He was fed up. He demanded that the corps head west—now! There was nothing Antoine could say to change the captain's mind.

The men scaled up and over a mountain, hiked through a ravine, then went along steep cliffs until they could go no farther. They were stuck. The only way they could escape was by lowering the wagons by rope from jagged rocks. Several wagons were destroyed, and Cooke's men were exhausted by the time they got across the mountain. From there, they pressed on through the desert until they reached San Diego.

Moses E. "California Joe" Milner, scouted for Lt. Col. George A. Custer's Seventh Cavalry. While Custer and his division were wiped out at the Little Bighorn, California Joe had sneaked off to prospect for gold.

Thousands of settlers and miners used this route to get to California for years afterward. Of course, they wisely traveled the extra day to cross the mountains at Guadalupe Pass. The trail was named after Captain Cooke, even though it was his scout, Antoine Leroux, who discovered the route.

Scouts in the Native American Wars

Another purpose of the army's Corps of Topographical Engineers was to locate Native Americans and inform the U.S. Cavalry of their whereabouts. The cavalry would then violently force the Native Americans off their land. For years scouts had led groups of white men *away* from Native Americans. Now their job was to lead them *to* the Native Americans.

Several army scouts were noted for their skill at finding Native Americans. Among them were Will Comstock, Lonesome Charley Reynolds, Luther "Yellowstone" Kelly, Frank Grouard, and Johnnie Bruguier.

Will Comstock

The business of guiding the army through the West was dangerous, yet scouts were paid little for their efforts. Will Comstock once led an army of men through a blizzard for two weeks. On the day he got the group to safety, he was fired.

However, Comstock was so knowledgeable that the army kept coming back to him. He worked most often with Lieutenant Colonel George Custer, who later gained fame in the Battle of the Little Bighorn. "He is a valuable man," the colonel wrote about Will, "and I am constantly learning valuable information from him regarding the Indians, their habits, etc."[1] There was nothing more to learn from Will after August 16, 1868. That is the date on which he was killed—shot from his saddle by Cheyenne warriors.

Lonesome Charley

Lonesome Charley Reynolds was once hired by the army to carry a report more than one hundred miles between two forts in the Black Hills. The danger was that the Dakota Territory was the home of the Sioux, who were being viciously attacked by the army. Lonesome Charley volunteered for the job. He traveled by night, and he hid with his horse in bushes during the day. The Sioux often passed so close that he could hear them talking, but they never caught him. He reached the fort safely, and he presented his report to the army commander.

Charley became so skilled at hunting elk, deer, and antelope for the army that Native Americans nicknamed him "Lucky Man." But he wasn't so lucky on June 25, 1876, when he guided Custer's Seventh Cavalry to the Little Bighorn River for a massive battle with Sioux and Cheyenne warriors led by Crazy Horse and Sitting Bull. Charley was among the hundreds of men killed that day; he was shot through the heart. The bloody battle became known as the Battle of the Little Bighorn.

Native Americans as Army Scouts

Colonel John Gibbon of the U.S. Seventh Infantry wrote of the Native American scout: "He knows every path, every pass in the mountains and every waterhole as thoroughly as the antelope or other wild animals which

Sergeant Red Tomahawk stands before the Standing Rock Reservation Indian Police. While arresting legendary chief, Sitting Bull, the Indian police encountered resistance from Sitting Bull's followers. After shooting began, Red Tomahawk fired the fatal shot that killed Sitting Bull.

Curley was another of Custer's Seventh Cavalry scouts, and one of the few survivors of the Little Bighorn. Some said, though, that Custer had sent him away before the battle began.

range through it. He knows exactly where he can go and where he cannot."[2]

Native Americans even scouted for the U.S. Army. Many Native Americans began to realize that the coming of the white settlers would not stop. Their land would never be the same again. Instead of fighting against this invasion, some Native Americans switched sides and began fighting for the U.S. government. And most were pleased to receive the pay of $13 a month. By 1866, about one thousand Native Americans were serving as scouts. Some of the greatest Native American scouts were Bloody Knife and a Crow scout named Curley, both of whom worked for Custer and the Apache Kid.

The Apache Kid

The Apache Kid helped the U.S. Army in a number of battles against the Apache leader Geronimo. The Kid was so respected by the army that he was elevated to the rank of first sergeant. After many years of loyal service, however, the Kid suddenly became a man hunted by the army. The Kid discovered that his father had been murdered. He wanted revenge. The Kid tracked down and killed one of his father's murderers. The Kid was later captured and sentenced to seven years in prison. He and his comrades, however, escaped on their way to jail. For years the Kid was hunted by his former coworkers, but was never found.

The Apache Kid (center) led the U.S. Army in its fight against the Apache.

⚔ 5 ⚔

JIM BRIDGER AND KIT CARSON

Kit Carson was thought by many to be the greatest scout ever. Others say the supreme scout was Jim Bridger. Both men contributed mightily to the exploration of the West, and both had plenty of memorable experiences along the way.

Jim Bridger

Bridger had learned the terrain of much of the West as a fur trapper and guide. He led large groups of trapping parties across the Great Plains, through the Rocky Mountains and the Sierra Nevada Mountains, and into California. When he came across lost travelers, he would use a piece of charcoal to draw a map of the region on a buffalo skin, and he would give it to the travelers to use as a guide. Sometimes he would pour handfuls of sand on a blanket to form mountains, using his fingertips to draw rivers. He seemed to know almost every hill and hollow throughout the West.

Bridger was so admired that he was given affectionate nicknames. A Bible-reading mountain man named Jedediah Smith said that Jim reminded him of the angel Gabriel, so Jedediah and his friends called him "Old Gabs." For parties and other special occasions, Jim would wear a colorful blue robe made for him by his Native American wife, so the Native Americans called him "Blanket Chief."

Jim liked to sit with friends around the campfire and tell them stories of his exciting life as a scout. Some of the stories were farfetched, while others were strange but true. Two of the mysterious places he liked to tell about were the river that flowed so swiftly that it got hot at the bottom, and the river that flowed in two opposite directions at once. Both of these wonders were real. One was the Fire Hole River, in what is today Yellowstone National Park. There an underground hot spring heats the water. The other was Two Ocean Creek in the Grand Teton Mountains of Wyoming. Many rivers split into two branches along a line known as the Continental Divide. At this line, one branch of Two Ocean Creek began to flow eastward down the mountain, while the other flowed westward down the other side.

Jim also could tell stories to the Native Americans, using sign language. He would point and gesture silently as his audience stared at his hands. They would occasionally gasp with fear, or laugh hysterically.

Jim didn't always get along with Native Americans, however. While he was scouting with a group of trappers in 1832, Jim's party came across a band of Blackfoot. One of the Blackfoot rode forward with a peace pipe,

Jim Bridger (1804–1881) was known as the scout's scout. He went on his first fur-trapping expedition in 1822. Later he built Fort Bridger in Wyoming Territory. It became an important stop for pioneers on the Oregon Trail.

and Jim came out to meet him halfway. It was a trick; the Blackfoot grabbed Jim's rifle and conked him over the head with it. A battle broke out that didn't end until nightfall. Nine Blackfoot and three trappers were killed. Jim was shot with arrows twice in one shoulder. His friends were able to remove one of the arrows, but they could only snap off the shaft of the other, leaving the arrowhead lodged in Jim's shoulder. Jim didn't have the second arrow removed until he saw a doctor three years later.

Jim demonstrated his keen eyesight one time while he was leading an Army expedition. He pointed out a thin column of smoke that was rising above some distant hills. The army general and his men could not see the smoke, even with the use of binoculars. Other scouts rode in later and told of a Native American village in the precise spot that Jim had pointed out.

Kit Carson

Kit Carson, like Jim Bridger, learned Native American ways at a young age. Kit lived in a log cabin in Missouri with his parents and four older brothers. By the time Kit was ten years old, he had learned to hunt with a rifle. He was friendly with Native Americans, and soon learned to speak their language. When Kit was twelve, he was given his first horse. He taught himself to shoot from the saddle, even while he was hanging under the horse. Finally, at the age of eighteen, Kit joined a group

Christopher "Kit" Carson (1809–1868). As a scout, Carson's treatment of Native Americans was sometimes brutal. However, he was later made superintendent of Indian Affairs for the Colorado Territory.

of settlers bound for New Mexico. He had become a frontiersman.

Over the next decade, Kit learned the ways of a scout. He could survive in the wilderness, and he could communicate with Native Americans through the use of sign language. Most important, he could "read sign," which meant that he could determine the general activity of the area by finding clues. Kit could examine streams, or grasses, or sand, or even tree bark, and figure out who had been there and when.

As gifted a scout as Kit was, he probably never would have become famous if it weren't for an explorer named John Charles Fremont. Likewise, Fremont never would have accomplished all he did without his main

pursue day and night an unknown body of Indians . . .
attack them on sight, without counting numbers . . . and
defeat them in an instant . . . and for what? To punish
the robbers of the desert and avenge the wrongs of
Mexicans."[1] Fremont failed to realize that Kit attacked
the Paiute to scare them. Kit hoped to discourage the
Paiute from attacking his own party. The plan worked.

For the next several years, Kit led expeditions
through the West. An army lieutenant who traveled
with Kit wrote: "Carson, while traveling, scarcely spoke;
his keen eye was continually examining the country. A
braver man than Kit perhaps never lived, in fact I doubt
if he knew what fear was."[2]

✴◀ 6 ▶✴

THE END OF THE SCOUT

———◆•◆•◆———

Two later scouts who achieved an even greater and more long-lasting fame were the two Bills: Buffalo Bill Cody and Wild Bill Hickok. Both were known throughout the Wild West by white settlers and Native Americans alike.

Cody was leading fifteen Fifth Cavalry soldiers one day when he spotted a group of Cheyenne coming up the trail. Cody signaled for the soldiers to hide in the weeds. As the Cheyenne approached, a shot rang out, and the fight was on. Three Cheyenne were immediately killed. The rest quickly escaped. The soldiers figured that the battle was over. All at once, the Cheyenne who were riding away turned around and attacked. In the midst of the fighting, the chief yelled out, "I know you, Pa-ho-has-ka! Come and fight with me!"[1] The chief was yelling to Buffalo Bill Cody. Pa-ho-has-ka meant "Long-Yellow Hair."

Buffalo Bill accepted the chief's challenge. He killed the chief's horse by shooting it with his rifle. Then his own horse stepped in a hole and fell. Now the two combatants stood face-to-face about twenty feet apart. They both fired at the same instant. The chief's bullet zipped past Bill's ear and Bill's shot hit the chief in the chest. The chief fell to the ground, and Bill finished him off with a knife. Bill would remember the bloody scene for the rest of his life.

Cody became a buffalo hunter in 1860 at the age of fourteen. He provided food for construction crews of the Kansas Pacific Railroad. He delivered so many buffalo carcasses to the crew that they called him "Buffalo Bill." Later that year, he became the youngest of eighty riders hired to carry the mail for the new Pony Express. Most

William F. "Buffalo Bill" Cody (1846–1917) as a young man.

of all, Bill was a scout. He worked for many years as a guide for the U.S. Army. Bill loved scouting so much that he named his only son Kit Carson Cody, in honor of the legendary scout.

Buffalo Bill was the chief of scouts for the Fifth Cavalry, and he was joined in 1868 by another crafty scout whose nickname was Wild Bill. The two Bills were similar in many ways. Both wore their hair down to their shoulders, both were expert shots, and both knew the terrain of the West as well as anyone.

Cody and Hickok worked side by side for the Fifth Cavalry until Hickok was attacked. He was scouting alone when he came across several Cheyenne and got into a running fight. A warrior got close enough to shove a spear through Hickok's thigh. When Cody found him the next morning, Hickok was near death. Dragging himself along the trail, he used the spear as a crutch. Cody brought his friend to an army surgeon, who saved his life and his leg.

Hickok moved to Kansas, where he served as sheriff of Hays City and later as marshal of Abilene. Cody also quit the scouting business and headed East. Neither man really wanted to stop working as a scout. The truth was that there just wasn't much use for scouts anymore.

Easterners predicted at the start of the nineteenth century that it would take five hundred years to settle the West; but they were wrong. The West was exploding

James B. "Wild Bill" Hickok (1837–1876) is well dressed for his job as a scout.

with growth, and the land was no longer a mystery. This meant the end for the scout.

As the 1800s wore on, trails once known only to Native Americans were becoming more and more familiar to new settlers from the East. Precise maps were being drawn, and guidebooks written. Mountains and streams were counted and mapped. The Wild West was being documented:

- ❖ When the Civil War broke out, armies began marching across America, carefully marking trails as they went.
- ❖ Thousands of miners scoured hills and hollows across the vast land in search of silver and gold.

As it was important to establish ownership of claims, these areas were accurately mapped.

❖ Railroad tracks were laid west clear to California. For those with money, traveling in wagon trains was no longer necessary.

❖ Telegraph lines were crisscrossed through the West like an enormous cobweb. Information passed more quickly from coast to coast.

❖ Native American territory shrank as settlers pushed west. Attacking war parties were no longer a risk in many areas. By 1890, the Native American wars were over.

As the nineteenth century came to a close, scouts continued to travel into the far reaches of the West, but for new reasons. Instead of guiding trappers, pioneers, or armies into unknown lands, scouts led sightseeing groups, hunting parties, and wealthy tourists who wanted a taste of the Wild West. Sometimes, dime novelists and photographers were brought along to record the trips as scouts told tales of their earlier exploits.

Buffalo Bill Cody was a master among tour guides. He found another occupation when his true scouting days came to an end. Since most Easterners were unable or unwilling to travel west, Cody brought the Wild West to them. Buffalo Bill became an actor in Wild West shows held in outdoor arenas throughout the East. He portrayed himself as a courageous scout who roamed the land. Wild Bill Hickok joined his friend as an actor in these shows, and the two Bills starred together as scouts.

Their friendship ended in 1876, when Hickok was

Buffalo Bill (center) and Wild Bill (second from left) teamed up in a Wild West show called "The Scouts of the Prairie" in 1872.

murdered while he was playing cards in a saloon. Wild Bill allegedly was holding a pair of aces and a pair of eights when the cards spilled from his hands. Ever since, the combination has been known as the Dead Man's Hand.

Buffalo Bill was crushed by his friend's death but he continued his acting career. For the next decade, Cody portrayed the life of the scout—drawing maps, foraging for food, hunting game, inspecting the ground for clues, battling Native Americans, guiding expeditions across the rugged land. It was all very exciting to his audiences. It could never be as exciting as it was to the scouts themselves, the men who blazed trails through the forbidding wilderness—the real scouts of the Wild West.

NOTES BY CHAPTER

Chapter 1
1. Harvey Lewis Carter, *"Dear Old Kit."* (Norman, Okla.: University of Oklahoma Press, 1968), p. 60.
2. Ibid, p. 61.

Chapter 2
1. Keith Wheeler, *The Scouts* (Alexandria, Va.: Time-Life Books, 1978), p. 15.

Chapter 4
1. Keith Wheeler, *The Scouts* (Alexandria, Va.: Time-Life Books, 1978), p. 88.
2. Phillip H. Stevens, *Search Out the Land* (Chicago: Rand McNally & Company, 1969), p. 103.

Chapter 5
1. Keith Wheeler, *The Scouts* (Alexandria, Va.: Time-Life Books, 1978), p. 26.
2. Ibid, p. 28.

Chapter 6
1. Phillip H. Stevens, *Search Out the Land* (Chicago: Rand McNally & Company, 1969), p. 98.

GLOSSARY

California Trail—The trail pioneers used to get to California. It followed the same route at the Oregon Trail before breaking off near Fort Hall (Idaho) and heading southwest to Sacramento.

cavalry—An army unit of soldiers mounted on horseback.

corps—A small army unit.

emigrants—People who leave their country or their home, and travel to another place to live.

frontiersman—In the Wild West, a person who has lived on the frontier and learned how to survive in the wilderness.

Oregon Trail—The trail pioneers took to get to Oregon. Most pioneers left from Independence, Missouri, heading northwest over the Great Plains. The trail crossed the Rockies at South Pass and continued northwest to the Willamette Valley.

ravine—A steep-sided valley.

reading sign—To examine streams, grasses, footprints and other signs in order to figure out who has recently been in a certain area.

scout—A person who stays ahead of a traveling group to make sure all is safe and clear ahead; they also look out for food, water, and shelter.

topographical—Relating to land surfaces, and prominent features such as mountains, valleys, and rivers.

✤◀ FURTHER READING ▶✤

Allen, John Loga. *Jedediah Smith and the Mountain Men of the American West.* New York: Chelsea House, 1991.

Blumber, Rhoda. *The Incredible Journey of Lewis and Clark.* New York: Lothrop, Lee & Shepard Books, 1987.

Brown, Marion Marsh. *Sacajawea: Indian Interpreter to Lewis and Clark.* Chicago: Children's Press, 1988

Burt, Olive Wooley. *Sacajawea, A Visual Biography.* New York: Watts, 1978.

Carter, Harvey Lewis. *"Dear Old Kit."* Norman, Okla.: University of Oklahoma Press, 1968.

Noonan, John. *Lewis and Clark.* New York: Crestwood House, 1993.

Stallones, Jared. *Zebulon Pike and the Explorers of the American Southwest.* New York: Chelsea House Publishers, 1992.

Syme, Ronald. *John Charles Fremont: The Last American Explorer.* New York: Morrow, 1974.

Wheeler, Keith. *The Scouts.* Alexandria, Va.: Time-Life Books, 1978.

INDEX

A

Abilene, Kansas, 40
Apache Indians, 29
Apache Kid, 28-29
Applegate, Jesse, 21
Applegate's Cutoff, 21

B

Battle of the Little Bighorn, 26
Blackfoot Indians, 32-33
Black Hills, 5-7, 26
Bloody Knife, 28
Boone, Daniel, 7
Bridger, Jim, 14, 30-33
Bruguier, Johnnie, 25

C

California Trail, 20-21
Carson, Kit, 5-7, 14, 30, 33-37
Cascade Mountains, 21
Charbonneau, Toussaint, 11
Cheyenne Indians, 26, 38-40
Civil War, 41
Clark, William, 10-12
Cody, Buffalo Bill, 38-43
Cody, Kit Carson, 40
Comstock, Will, 25-26
Continental Divide, 32
Cooke, Philip, 23-25
Corps of Topographical Engineers, 22
Crazy Horse, 26
Crow Indians, 28

Curley, 28
Custer, George A., 26

D

Declaration of Independence, 7
Dodge, Grenville, 15-16
duties of scouts, 13-14

F

Fifth Cavalry, 38, 40
Fitzpatrick, Thomas (Broken Hand), 17-20
Fort Bridger, 31
Fremont, John Charles, 34-37

G

Geronimo, 29
Gibbon, John, 27
Godey, Alexis, 35-37
Grand Teton Mountains, 32
Great Plains, 30
Greenwood, Caleb, 20-21
Gros Ventre Indians, 17-20
Grouard, Frank, 25
Guadalupe Pass, 24-25

H

Harris, Moses, 21
Hays City, Kansas, 40
Hickok, Wild Bill, 38, 40, 43
Hitchcock, Isaac, 20-21

K

Kansas Pacific Railroad, 39

Kelly, Luther Yellowstone, 25

L
Leroux, Antoine, 22-25
Lewis, Merriwether, 10-12
Long, Stephen H., 11-12

M
Mexicans, 35, 37
Mojave Desert, 14, 35

N
Native Americans, 8-10, 13, 17-21, 25-29, 32-40, 42-43

O
Oregon Trail, 21

P
Paiute Indians, 35-37
Pike, Zebulon, 11
Pilgrims, 8
Pony Express, 39

R
Revolutionary War, 8

Reynolds, Lonesome Charley, 25-27
Rocky Mountains, 14, 17, 23-24, 30, 36

S
Sacajawea, 10-12
San Diego, California, 23-25
Sante Fe, New Mexico, 23
Shoshone Indians, 11
Sierra Nevada Mountains, 21, 30
Sioux Indians, 26
Smith, Jedediah, 31
Stevens, Elisha, 20-21

U
Union Pacific Railroad, 15
U.S. Cavalry, 25

W
Wilderness Road, 7

Y
Yellowstone National Park, 32